Hayley the Halloween Cat & the Search for Bitty the Bat

by
Wanda Luthman

Hayley the Halloween Cat
&
the Search for Bitty the Bat

Copyright (C) 2018 by Wanda Luthman

All rights reserved solely by the author. The author guarantees all contents are original and do not infringe upon the legal rights of any other person or work. No part of this book may be reproduced or transmitted, by any means, without permission from the author.

ISBN: 978-0-9981958-6-5

Library of Congress: 2018911917

For more intofrmation please visit:

www.wandaluthman.wordpress.com

www.facebook.com/wluthman

Her friend, Torpedo, the large gray rat, asked, "Have you looked under the welcome mat?" Hayley replied, "Yes, but he wasn't there. I can't find him anywhere."

"Did you check under the scarecrow's hat?"
asked the plump little pumpkin named Pat.
But before Hayley could take a peek,
a starling named Jack poked out his beak.

Hayley cried, "That's not Bitty, my friend.
Oh, when will this crazy search ever end?"
The fuzzy twin spiders named Spit and Spat
asked, "Have you looked under the witch's vat?"

Hayley's eyes grew wide with fear.
"Surely he'd never hide under there!"
She hurried over and looked under the pot.
Thank goodness there was just an empty spot.

"What about the scientist's lab?" asked the friendly monster named Dibbity-Dab. Hayley squeaked open the old wooden door searching for Bitty the bat once more.

In the corner, the skeleton shook his rickety bones and said, "Maybe he wants to be alone?"
Hayley sighed. "How can that be?
Doesn't he want to play with me?"

"So, you've checked the hat, the mat, and the vat?" asked the friendly ghost, Mr. Tatterdy-Tat. Hayley nodded her head and said, "I even checked up under the bed."

My friend, the bat, is nowhere to be seen.
I guess he's going to miss this Halloween."
Just as the sun started sinking low
and Hayley's tears began to flow,

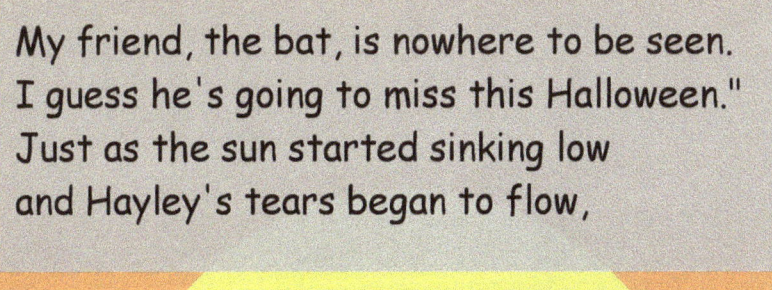

a speck came flying in all ziggity-zat.
It was Bitty, the little acrobat.
Everyone cheered when they saw their friend.
Then, Hayley asked, "Where have you been?"

Now look up here if you're ready to see
the magic show... starring ME!"
The night sky was dark as Bitty took flight.
His friends were amazed at the wondrous sight.

Bitty's wings were all aglow
as he put on a real acrobatic show.
Everyone laughed and danced and cheered,
knowing now, why Bitty had disappeared.

Hayley the Halloween cat
hugged her best friend, Bitty the bat.
"I thought you were going to miss the Halloween fun,
but now the party has really begun!"

Also by Wanda Luthman

www.ingramcontent.com/pod-product-compliance
Lightning Source LLC
Chambersburg PA
CBHW051555010526
44118CB00022B/2715